Read for a Better World™

I0090311

BULLDOZERS

A First Look

ZELDA WAGNER

Lerner Publications ◆ Minneapolis

Educator Toolbox

Reading books is a great way for kids to express what they're interested in. Before reading this title, ask the reader these questions:

What do you think this book is about? Look at the cover for clues.

What do you already know about bulldozers?

What do you want to learn about bulldozers?

Let's Read Together

Encourage the reader to use the pictures to understand the text.

Point out when the reader successfully sounds out a word.

Praise the reader for recognizing sight words such as *on* and *in*.

TABLE OF CONTENTS

Bulldozers

Bulldozers are strong. They push dirt and other things. They clear land.

What else might bulldozers push?

Most bulldozers drive on tracks. Tracks grip the earth.

Bulldozers have drivers. A driver sits in the cab.

A bulldozer pushes dirt with its blade.

The blade is
on the front.

The bulldozer makes a smooth path. It clears the way for a new road.

Why do roads need a smooth path?

What else might a ripper dig?

Some bulldozers have a ripper. A ripper digs up soil to make a ditch.

A bulldozer clears trees in the woods. Now workers can build a house.

Some bulldozers
move trash.

Others push snow.

STEM Snapshot

Encourage students to think and ask questions like scientists. Ask the reader:

What is something you learned about bulldozers?

What is something you noticed about bulldozer parts?

What is something you still want to learn about bulldozers?

Photo Glossary

blade

path

ripper

tracks

Learn More

Jaske, Julia. *Look, a Bulldozer!* Ann Arbor, MI: Cherry Lake, 2021.

Loy, Harriet. *A Bulldozer's Day*. Minneapolis: Bellwether Media, 2023.

Wagner, Zelda. *Concrete Mixers: A First Look*. Minneapolis: Lerner Publications, 2025.

Index

Photo Acknowledgments

Image credits: Bogdanhoda/Getty Images, p. 5; Chris Jongkind/Getty Images, p. 6; Pro-syanov/Getty Images, p. 7; Deekens/Getty Images, p. 8; Fertnig/Getty Images, p. 10; fotog/Getty Images, p. 11; Maksim Safaniuk/Shutterstock, p. 13; poco_bw/Getty Images, p. 14; asadykov/Getty Images, p. 15; alekseystemmer/Getty Images, p. 17; WALTER ZERLA/Getty Images, p. 18; kellymarken/Getty Images, p. 19; moodboard/Getty Images, p. 20.
Cover: Bogdanhoda/Getty Images.

Lerner Publications Company
An imprint of Lerner Publishing Group, Inc.
241 First Avenue North
Minneapolis, MN 55401 USA

For reading levels and more information, look up this title at www.lernerbooks.com.

Main body text set in Mikado Medium.
Typeface provided by Hannes von Doehren.

Library of Congress Cataloging-in-Publication Data

Names: Wagner, Zelda, 2000- author.
Title: Bulldozers : a first look / Zelda Wagner.
Description: Minneapolis : Lerner Publications, [2025] | Series: Read about construction vehicles | Includes bibliographical references and index. | Audience: Ages 5–8 | Audience: Grades K–1 | Summary: "Bulldozers drive, push, and dig. Some even have a ripper! Readers learn more about these exciting construction vehicles and how they work"—Provided by publisher.
Identifiers: LCCN 2024006402 (print) | LCCN 2024006403 (ebook) | ISBN 9798765647813 (lib. bdg.) | ISBN 9798765662199 (pbk.) | ISBN 9798765657157 (epub)
Subjects: LCSH: Bulldozers—Juvenile literature.
Classification: LCC TA735 .W3425 2025 (print) | LCC TA735 (ebook) | DDC 629.225—dc23/eng/20240304

LC record available at https://lccn.loc.gov/2024006402
LC ebook record available at https://lccn.loc.gov/2024006403

Manufactured in the United States of America
1-1010887-53342-4/25/2024